STUDY HACKS FOR COLLEGE STUDENTS

Effective Study Hacks to Help Save Time and Get Better Grades

CHANIN STORM

Dragon Alchemy Publishing

STUDY HACKS FOR COLLEGE STUDENTS

To request permissions, contact the publisher at projectcoordinator@dragonalchemypublishing.com.

Paperback: 978-1-7377292-2-8
eBook: 978-1-7377292-3-5

Library of Congress Number: 2021953507

First Edition January 2022.

Printed by Ingram in the USA.

Dragon Alchemy Publishing
Frederick, MD 21701

Dragonalchemypublishing.com

ACKNOWLEDGEMENTS

This book was 10 years in the making and many people were a part of its creation. While I can't thank them all, I do want to make sure I mention a few of the people that were a large part of this book being published.

First, I want to thank my mother. She always supports my endeavors even when it is changing careers in my 40s. She never blinked an eye. When I told her I was going to write a book, she had only words of encouragement and belief in my ability.

I also want to thank my second sets of eyes. My beta team and ARC readers, you all were the best. My editor/proofreader, Denise, for the hard work polishing the chapters and making sure I was on point.

Thank you to especially the students, to whom I used to learn this information as much as teach over the last 10 years. Thank you all for giving me feedback and making the information in the book as relevant as possible.

Thank you all!

CONTENTS

Everyone wants to have an excellent education, but no one wants to study. We do it to get the diploma, degree, certificate, we have to pass exams, write papers, do projects, and so many other things to say we have that excellent education. But how often do we push off studying because friends want to come over or go out? How many times do we say, "I'll read that tomorrow" or "I'll research that Saturday" because a good show is coming on TV? Most of us have done all of these at least once, if not 100 times.

I am as much a part of this group of excuse-makers as anyone else. In high school, I would avoid taking my books home and hated studying. I did the bare minimum in college, usually the night before, just to get something turned in. However, the process changed a little when children entered the picture. I knew I couldn't just skim by anymore. My actions would be served as consequences to my children. I'll admit it. I tried to change my ways, and I did study a little more. I can remember only one project being left to the very last day during my senior year in college. Other projects were usually two or three days before the due date, so I will admit I didn't change that much. What changed was why I put off studying. I had to care for my daughter. I had to work. I wanted a life. Name it; I had an excuse.

When I returned to college several years after my second child was born, it was even harder to study. I had fallen out of even the basic study habits and had to relearn them all over. However, this time, I had some experience in life and the workforce that helped me out. Eventually, I earned my Master's degree and started teaching. You know what I discovered my first semester teaching at the local community college? No one is really ever taught how to study. I had never thought about that as a teen or young adult. We are told to take notes, read the text, research, or whatever, but no one really teaches how to do these things to ensure you are using your time effectively and getting the most needed information.

I went on to create personal development courses that help people learn to study. I had classes focused on middle school and high school students, college students, and adults who had been out of education for a while and needed a refresher on studying. At first, people laughed, but when I continued to have students sign up and parent sign up their kids, I knew I had to share this with everyone.

There is a science to learning based on how our brains work. Yes, we are all individuals, but the brain still pretty much basically functions in the same way. We just have different thoughts.

This book will touch on that a little because I am not a scientist – I hold Political Science, English Language, and Literature and Creative Writing degrees - notice no science or math. However, in education, there is little that can be said about how the brain works when we study. This is what the book will touch on. However, the most significant portion of this book is to help you learn to study effectively and efficiently without having your nose in your textbooks all the time.

Here's a teaser. I tell my students to never study the night before an exam! I had a few angry parents come to talk to me when I told their children that one. The best part is that when you follow what I lay out in this book, you won't need to study the night before, and you will still get great grades.

What are study hacks? We have all heard about hacks since the internet was born. We see hacks for home, wardrobe, cars, buying, selling

- you name it, there is a hack. So why shouldn't studying have a hack! In today's world, corner-cutting is too much of the norm. Unfortunately, you are often cutting out vital information when you cut corners. When you learn these study hacks, you get the information while cutting corners, so it is a win-win situation. These are hacks I have used personally for over 20 years and that I have taught for over a decade. They work, and they are easier than you can imagine. Don't think of these hacks as the easy way to learn because that is not the case. You still have to be active in the studying process; you just don't have to eat, sleep, live, dream, studying all the time.

Using the five processes in this book will help you study more effectively, efficiently, and be more confident in knowing the information. So let's stop playing around and procrastinating. Let's get started.

Chapter 1: Calendars & Project Time Lines

In this chapter, we will talk about getting organized. Living in the academic world thinking that you will just follow the syllabus or do whatever the teacher tells you to do is fine, and you will survive, but you will not thrive or work effectively and efficiently. You will always be a little behind. That is why it is so important to get organized and set goals from the start. In addition, you need to follow up on the goals and calendar, especially when things change, such as snow days, holidays, and such. We will detail the importance of calendars and use the goal setting template to help schedule activities for projects. I have a book all about setting goals, and we will be using the template from that book but will not be going into detail about goal setting. But let's first get started with the calendar.

Calendars Are Necessary

Truth be told, it took me a long time to believe that calendars were necessary for school and at work. But I learned fast that if I wanted to bring my "A" game to the classroom, I had to have my calendar in order. In today's world, that is easier than ever. We have hard copy planners and digital planners, so there are tons of options. The most important part of the calendar is actually using it.

I'm sure most people who just read the last paragraph will say that filling out a calendar is just a waste of time. Some people only write what they deem the most important parts of the week in their calendar. However, doing that, especially when trying to balance school and life, can lead to frustration and missing assignments. Every action in the class is important. Trust me. As a professor for almost a decade, everything I put on the syllabus was important to the grade. This included reading, assignments, quizzes, exams, papers, and every other stupid activity I included in my syllabus. Yes, I had students tell me some of the activities were stupid, but they learned valuable information from those stupid activities. Most even agreed that the stupid activities taught them things.

In many instances, your teachers and professors know exactly what you need to know to pass the class, and that is what they focus on during lectures and in every assignment they give you. I was right there with you in high school and most of college. I thought some of the assignments were just not that important. Why turn in an outline? Let me just write the paper. Why do a group project? I could do it better on my own. Why? Why? Why?

The answer is that many of your teachers and professors are not just teaching you about the objectives for the class but how to deal with situations in life. This is why learning to use a calendar now while you are in school is so important. If you are reading this as a returning adult student, you know what I am saying is true. You miss a deadline at work and that could mean your job or loss of a promotion. Calendars are extremely important in school and work, so learn how to use them now and make your adult life much easier.

How To Use A Calendar

A calendar can be beautiful, but all it does is show the date. Yes, that is the purpose of calendars, but the calendar is not very useful as a calendar, or rather it is not used to its full potential unless there are items written on the important dates. Maybe you use a digital calendar on your phone or computer. I bet it still looks pristine and clean with few to no appointments or deadlines on it. Think about how often you use your calendar. Then think of how many times you have rushed because you almost forgot an appointment or worked late because you almost forgot a deadline. Having a calendar in your face will alleviate that stress and last-minute rush.

Calendars should be used to ensure that we don't miss appointments, deadlines, classes, and so much more. A clean, pristine calendar is just paper with dates on it, but a beautifully written on and highlighted weekly calendar is so much more and will make your world more efficient. Did you see that I mentioned "highlighted" in the previous sentence? That's right. To make your calendar more effective, you should highlight every appointment, due date, and anything else you have written on it. For hard copy calendars, this is where highlighter markers come into play. For digital calendars, it is just as easy but less messy.

Let's look at a student calendar -

EXAMPLE

WEEKLY PLANNER

SUNDAY	MONDAY	TUESDAY	WEDNESDAY	THURSDAY	FRIDAY	SATURDAY
1:30pm - 2:00pm English Study Time 2:00pm - 2:30pm English Study Time 3:00pm - 3:30pm Science Study Time 3:30pm - 4:00pm Science Study Time 4:30pm - 5:00pm History Study Time 5:00pm - 5:30pm History Study Time	**10:00am - 10:50am** **English Class** **11:30am - 1:00pm** **Science Class/Lab** 2:00pm - 2:30pm Art History Study Time 2:30pm - 3:00pm Art History Study Time **5:00pm - 5:50pm** **History Class**	**10:30am - 11:45am** **Art History Class** 1:30pm - 2:00pm English Study Time 2:00pm - 2:30pm English Study Time 3:00pm - 3:30pm Science Study Time 3:30pm - 4:00pm Science Study Time 4:30pm - 5:00pm History Study Time 5:00pm - 5:30pm History Study Time	**10:00am - 10:50am** **English Class** **11:30am - 1:00pm** **Science Class/Lab** 2:00pm - 2:30pm Art History Study Time 2:30pm - 3:00pm Art History Study Time **5:00pm - 5:50pm** **History Class**	**10:30am - 11:45am** **Art History Class** 1:30pm - 2:00pm English Study Time 2:00pm - 2:30pm English Study Time 3:00pm - 3:30pm Science Study Time 3:30pm - 4:00pm Science Study Time 4:30pm - 5:00pm History Study Time 5:00pm - 5:30pm History Study Time	**10:00am - 10:50am** **English Class** **11:30am - 1:00pm** **Science Class/Lab** **5:00pm - 5:50pm** **History Class**	**Rest Day - No Studying**

This is a real calendar of a college student with classes on Monday, Wednesday, and Friday. He has given each class a specific color and has even scheduled the times to have the activities done on the days he is in school. This is a great start and shows how, with a calendar, the student can effectively keep on top of reading assignments, projects, and deadlines. We can see that our example student reviews the chapter with the lecture notes right after his Art class. Then he does his Math homework right after math class. While it doesn't show much for the English class on the days he has class, it does show that he works on things for English and Art on the days he is not in class. These are the classes that normally have extra projects and activities.

Can you see how the calendar is beautiful in its own way? Can you identify with the calendar as a way to stay on top of everything you need to do to know when you have to get it done? The best part is when you use a calendar and project timeline, you can build in wiggle room in case you have to work, have a family gathering, or some other event that you have to attend. Planning your day out based on what is coming up in the future reduces stress in your life.

Are you ready to be less stressed and more organized? I bet you are, but this is not the only thing that needs to be done. We need to take the projects that the teacher or professor gives and put them into the calendar. Sometimes the instructor gives all project assignments or writing assignments at the beginning of the semester or term in a syllabus. Sometimes these assignments are given to students as the last project is completed to ensure the students only work on one assignment at a time. Either way, there is an easy way to create a project timeline to plop into the calendar and keep yourself on schedule.

Right now, put the book down, take out your syllabus if you have one, or your class schedule, and start creating the calendars. Each class should be a different color so that it is easy to see and can be differentiated from other classes, assignments, and appointments. Once you have the classes and due dates for all assignments, pick the book back up and learn about how to make a project timeline.

The Project Timeline

Creating a project timeline is very simple. No, you don't need an extra app or software. It is easily created with pen and paper or on a computer. Once you get the hang of it, even the most complex projects can be reduced to steps and the timeline created in a matter of minutes. So, let's get started.

You have probably already put your due date on the calendar, or at least you should have. However, if you wanted to get this information out of the way first, I completely understand. This process has you start with the assignment's final due date and then work backward to the day you receive the assignment. Each milestone in the assignment is another small step you put on the calendar. Then you break down the small steps to find out what you need to do to finish each step.

The project timeline template is one (1) Final Assignment and three (3) Small Assignments. You can add more Small Assignments if needed. You also don't have to use all three. The choice is yours, but I like to add a Small Assignment as each milestone for the Final Assignment.

For this example, we will use a prompt I used in one of the research classes I taught. The research paper was worth 30% of the students' grade for the semester. The full writing prompt is in Appendix B, along with a completed project timeline. A blank project timeline is in Appendix C. But for now, let's look at the assignment in pieces. The topics to choose from included the freedom of press, freedom of religion, or freedom of speech. It was an 8-10 page paper showing the student's ability to engage in civic and/or global relevance issues meaningfully. They needed 12 sources (7 scholarly journals, three other sources, one TedTalk, and one video shown in class of Martin Luther King Jr. giving his "I Have A Dream" Speech). They were given more instructions and told that all aspects of the assignment were part of the grade, except for the peer review, which meant their grade would be affected if they missed a due date. The assignment also included due dates for each of the assignment's milestones and how to submit that portion of the assignment. Please note for this assignment, the school used a learning management system (LMS) called Blackboard. There are many different

LMS applications out there, but for this example, Blackboard is used. When constructing the project timeline, we will start with the due dates:

Due Date for Thesis & Outline: November 9 by midnight on Blackboard
Peer Review: November 14 in class with hard copy
Due Date for Rough Draft: November 21 by 4 pm in hard copy and on Blackboard
Conference Dates: November 28 – December 2, 2016
Due Date for Final Essay: December 5 by 4 pm in hard copy and on Blackboard

The first thing we have to do is find the final due date, which is December 5 by 4 pm in hard copy and on Blackboard. The Final Assignment due date is December 5th. The Final Assignment may look something like the following:

EXAMPLE

Final Assignment: 8-10 page double spaced paper in APA format. The reference sheet and Title page are not included in the page count. I can use only 8 quotes in total. There must be 12 academic credible sources to include 2 videos (one of which is the MLK Jr. "I Have a Dream" speech), 3 other sources of my choosing, and 7 scholarly journals. I have to write in an academic tone and ensure my paper is free of grammatical errors and spelling errors. This will need time to research and create a logical, organized, well-thought-out research essay proving the point of my chosen topic and stance.

Deadline: December 5 by 4pm in hard copy to the professor's office and on Blackboard

Notice that everything the student needed is in the Final Assignment section of the project timeline, including the final submission date and location. We now turn our attention to the Small Assignments. Since the Peer Review doesn't count toward the grade, it is up to you as to whether you want to include it or not. I had my students include everything because it just makes more sense. If they missed their conference, they missed a one-on-one meeting with me where they could review their paper and get more insight from me about what they needed to do to get an "A" paper. I did not reschedule these conferences. So while they do not count toward the grade officially, missing one could affect the student's grade.

After the Final Assignment is on the project timeline, we start adding the Small Assignments. For this example, the following are included:

EXAMPLE

Small Assignment #1: Conference with Professor
Small Assignment #2: Rough draft Submission
Small Assignment #3: Prepare a draft for in-class peer review
Small Assignment #4: Prepare an outline with a thesis statement for submission

---

Notice that each of these Small Assignments corresponds to a due date in the writing assignment. This way, we will not miss anything and know where we stand with each step of the project. Also, notice that the Small Assignments start with the last step and end with the first step. Since our Final Assignment is at the top of the template, it just makes sense to work backward, marking off the Small Assignments as we go.

Next, we break these Small Assignments into steps and give each step a due date. We will use Small Assignment 4 for this example.

EXAMPLE

Small Assignment #4: Prepare an outline with a thesis statement for submission

Step 1 to reach Small Assignment #4: Research and choose my topic **Deadline for Step 1**: November 1

Step 2 to reach Small Assignment #4: Schedule an appointment at the Writing Center **Deadline for Step 2**: November 5

Step 3 to reach Small Assignment #4: Create my outline and thesis statement and include a basic reference sheet **Deadline for Step 3**: November 7

Remember, you can add more steps if needed. This Small Assignment had two extra steps added to ensure that all steps were included. Can you see how this can help you really strategize how you attack your projects? Think about it. This assignment was due in just over a month, so it was a lot of work in a short amount of time. Having this project timeline set up allowed the student to be more effective and efficient in their time. They knew when they would need to spend extra time on the assignment and what days would work with their project timeline. In addition, by doing this for every project, you keep on top of them all. You will have multiple projects in high school and college due at similar times. This can happen in the work world too, so college is just getting you ready for the real world. I can guarantee you, the teacher or professor will not want to hear that you had another project due, so that is why you haven't done the one they assigned. Using this template and the strategies in this chapter will keep you from having this talk with your instructor.

Once you have the project timeline complete, you add these due dates to your calendar. The calendar will start to look like a rainbow with a variety of colors every day. It will be beautiful in its structured chaos. It will also be even more beautiful when it helps you keep ahead of the game, turn in assignments on time, and begin to feel more confident in your academic career.

If you haven't done so already, now is the time to get your calendar and any timelines/syllabi from teachers and put them into the calendar. Then create project timelines for each and every project you have information on at this time. If you aren't sure of the actual requirements, set up the project timeline with the basics and the final due date for now. When you get the requirements, you can finish the project timeline and add the information to your calendar.

Updating Your Project Time Lines and Calendar

I stated earlier that you should review your calendars often. This is very true. Instructors get sick; schools close due to snow or other events; you get sick. So many things in life can wreak havoc on our schedules. Therefore, you should make it a habit to review your calendar and project timelines at least once a week. Since you don't study on Sunday, take 30 minutes to review the upcoming week and make sure you are on schedule for everything coming due. If you have missed a class or class was canceled and due dates have changed, this is the time to update your calendar and project timelines so that you can stay on schedule even when you are thrown a curveball. It really doesn't take much time, and it so worth it in the end.

Once you have your calendar ready and have project timelines in place for your upcoming school projects, it is time to move into the real hacks of how to study more effectively and efficiently in less time than you can imagine.

Chapter 2: It's Easy to Concentrate

We are all told that if we concentrate and study hard, we will get an "A" in the class. When we achieve less than an "A," many of us beat ourselves up and say things like: I should have concentrated more in class, I should have concentrated more while studying, or both or worse. But what is concentration really? We can concentrate on a book, video game, song, class. But that doesn't answer our question. What does concentration really mean? Concentration is the act of focusing your thoughts on only one topic/thing during a given time span. So, you can concentrate on a book while reading it as long as you aren't doing anything else. The same is true for a game, song, or class. It is literally giving your undivided attention to the thing in front of you.

This sounds pretty hard and/or boring when you think of this in terms of studying, doesn't it? The truth is that most of us will not be able to give our undivided attention completely, but that doesn't mean we aren't concentrating. We are concentrating to the best of our abilities. There are a few ways that we can make the "best of our abilities" a little closer to the undivided attention and really have less to do with concentration and more to do with location and time management.

You are probably thinking, this should have been in the previous chapter, but the fact is that it shouldn't. The last chapter showed you how to set up time management, but there is more to it than just putting in a calendar. In this chapter, the two things we will discuss are the study space and how to actually study and not just go through the actions. These are not the techniques to use when studying but the act of studying itself so that it is the most time-efficient and effective for you. This part may be the most important in terms of putting the rest of the strategies to work. Without this information, the other parts of this book are just ways to study but will not be as effective. The information in this chapter brings it all together, and allows you to study less and study better for better results in class.

Study Space

How many times have you grabbed your books and sat in front of the TV to study? Or maybe you go to the kitchen and spread out on the table, only to realize that you forgot your highlighter or notebook in another room. How many times have you set up your study time only to spend more time setting up than actually studying? I guarantee you, most of us have done all of these. These activities and others that are similar waste time and usually frustrate us to the point that we don't really study. In fact, we spend more time prepping for study and realizing that we don't have everything we need, so we give up, or we only study in a half-hearted way.

For the above reasons, you need to create a study space that is only for studying. This space doesn't have to be a separate room, and it doesn't have to be a permanent feature in the home. What it does have to do is be is a quiet space for your study time. This chapter explains how to set up this space and helps you decide its location to serve its purpose most effectively.

Location, Location, Location

You may have heard this phrase before - location, location, location. Everything is about location. The right location for a business will be the success or failure of that business. Being in the right location for a person trying to break into film or TV is imperative for being "discovered." Getting the manuscript in the hands of the right agent or publisher (the location is a person here) helps create new best-selling novelists. Everything that can be a success or a failure can pretty much be based on location. The same is true for studying.

Let's consider what is needed for the optimal study location. I've started the list, but I'm sure you may think about some other necessities of the space. This is not about what you need to study, but what you need in an area to allow you to have everything you need to study.

- Space
- Quiet

Sometimes we can think of other things; other times, we can't. For me, the only requirements I need are space to spread out a little - have an open textbook and a notebook or laptop for taking notes. How much space is this? Not really a lot is needed, but thinking about it makes you look at areas in your house that would work for you. Why? Because not everyone can have a separate room that is just for them to study. If you have that room - AWESOME! If not, still AWESOME, but you have to be a little more imaginative.

My other requirement is quiet so that I can think without interruption. How many times have you sat down at the dining room table to study and have a brother or sister run through the room screaming for some unknown reason? Or have your child ask for a snack when you just finished giving them one to keep them occupied because you want to study? Or a partner that doesn't understand why you have to study? Yes, we all have interruptions, and we will talk about this a little later. For now, think about the space you can use that will be "mostly" quiet if not wholly quiet.

So how many places in your house fit this description? There are three in my world, but that is because I have other information you'll be getting in a few minutes. For now, do any areas in your home fit the bill?

You may have thought of a place or two or maybe five; all are great. However, was one of those places you thought about automatically as having the space and quiet you need your bed? Well, get that thought out of your mind. Take that location off of your list. Have you ever grown tired while studying on your bed and fallen asleep? Exactly. Most of us have, and some of us have woken up with highlighter on our face to prove it. Your bed is not a good space to study. Let's find another place.

Any of the following will suffice for a space to study if you do not have an extra room in your house: a corner of a bedroom, dining room table, coffee table in a living or family room, or even a closet.

You're probably thinking, these places aren't quiet. Well, this is where the next step comes into play. This is where you write up a contract with your family or roommates to get them onboard with your studying. I guarantee most parents and family members will not deny this request. There are two copies of the contract at the end of the book in Appendix A. One is for people still living at home with their parents, and the other is for the adult living with a spouse and/or children or roommates. However, here is a sample of one of them.

Sample Contract

I, Johnny Smith, have concluded that I need 2 hours daily to sit quietly and study. I would like to do this every day, Monday through Friday, from 4:00 pm to 6:00 pm. On Saturdays, my study times will be from 10:00 am to 12:00 pm. I have created a study space at the dining room table and would appreciate this area to be a quiet zone on those days and times. I will not leave my studying on the table but will bring it to the table 5 minutes before the scheduled time and remove it within 5 minutes at the end of the scheduled time. I would also be willing to do chores before and/or after the scheduled time but would appreciate not being asked to do chores during the scheduled time. I feel that creating this study space and study schedule is being proactive in ensuring I have good grades throughout the school year. If you agree with my requested schedule, please sign below.

_Johnny Smith______________________________9/12/2020____

_Stephanie Smith___________________________9/12/2020____
Family Member/Roommate

If those who live with you see that you are really invested in this, they will help you any way they can. This doesn't mean that they will forget and talk to you or ask you to do something during your study time, but they will understand when you answer that you will do it after your study time has ended.

Honestly, I have had a few parents get a little upset about this contract when I send it home with students in my study skills class. Still, the truth is that after the students start implementing these strategies discussed in this book, they were more than willing to not only abide by the contract but help ensure that others did too - meaning brothers and sisters.

Now that we have the contract and everyone agrees that this is a great proactive way of getting through the school year let's revisit where your study locations can be. List them out. Take a picture of them or draw them, yes, even if it is the corner of a room with no furniture. It is now time to be creative and start really setting up the space.

If you have a desk in the corner of your room, you are set. But if you don't, the only thing you need is a sturdy box or tote. I prefer a tote because it lasts longer. In the tote, you will put all the things that you will need to set up your study space no matter where it is located. If you are at a table, you'll take the items out of the tote and put them on the table. If you are in a bare corner of your room, you take all the items out, put the lid back on the tote, and BAM, you have your desk for your notebook or laptop and the floor spread out on.

You are probably wondering what I mean when I say, "take the items out of the tote." What items do I mean? I hope that to save your back, you do not have everything in your backpack because I know that not everything is used every day. The only things that should be in your backpack are two to three pens and pencils, one highlighter, the notebooks for the classes on that day, and the textbooks for those same classes. Everything else should be in the tote. In the tote, you will have:

- a stapler
- tape dispenser with tape

- paper clips
- extra pens and pencils
- set of highlighters of different colors
- extra notebooks/paper
- maybe a desk lamp, if your corner or area doesn't have good lighting.

Can you think of anything else you might need? Some classes have specific items, so make sure you think about what you need for each class and include those items with this set of basic study items.

Now you have everything you need to create a study space, but before we move to the next topic, I want you to think about what you need to bring home every day to make this study space work for you. **Do** bring home the texts and information from the classes you attended that day. Those are the only items you will be using during the study time that day. **Do Not** bring home the texts for the classes the next day, even if there will be a test. If you follow this book's strategies, you won't need to have "cram" sessions.

A wise professor told me while I was in college cramming for an exam outside of his classroom, "If you don't know it by now, you won't for the test. You're just wasting your time and mine." This stuck with me, and I realized that he was right. From that day on, I never crammed for an exam, and I still rocked my grades. It is really about using your time wisely and effectively to ensure that you know the stuff well before the exam. It is about creating a habit of studying that will help you study less and rock your grades.

Bring home the textbooks, notes, and any handouts from the classes on that day. That is what you will be focused on that evening. If you have the same classes every day, it is a little different. Bring the books home every day for the first week, and then you will start to know the rhythm of classes and know when projects are due to help you better decide what is needed every evening.

Now is the fun part! Draw your study space. This not for anyone but you to start creating the space that will be the best for you to study. You can be outrageous and draw your optimal space, or you can draw what you have. This is a way to make your study space your own. Once you draw it out, get the tote and all the items. Mark the tote as your "Study Tote." If you study in the corner of your room, place the tote there. If you study in the dining room or another room in the house, put the tote in your room and carry it to the study room each day. Remember your contract - 5 minutes before the start time, you set up, and you will clean up within 5 minutes of your ending time.

Cramming

How often have you sat down the night before an exam and studied until the early hours of the morning, then gone to school feeling tired and unmotivated to take that exam you just "crammed" for all night? You probably did OK, but if you need that information for a later class or text, can you easily remember it? Probably not, and that is because cramming doesn't work for long term memory, **AND** whatever you have crammed for, you probably only remember a portion of what you think you did for the test.

Let's be honest here. **Cramming doesn't work!** It just doesn't. It is one of the worst things a student can do when studying for an exam.

When I was a sophomore in college, I was outside of my criminal justice classroom cramming for the midterm exam. My professor stopped in front of me and looked down at where I sat on the floor. What he said next has stayed with me since that day, and as soon as he said those words, I knew they were true. What did he say?

"If you don't know it now, you won't know it for the exam, so don't bother studying anymore."

I was floored. Yet, I knew he was right and that I was never going to retain anything that wasn't already in my brain at that point. I closed my book, stood up, and went in to take the test. I had studied diligently prior to the exam, so I passed it with an "A," but the truth is we are conditioned to study up until the moment we take that exam. We are conditioned to cram every bit of knowledge about a topic into our brain for the test the night before or the morning of the exam. It is what we are told to do and what we are expected to do. **But in reality, I'll say it again, cramming doesn't work.**

So what does work? Using the studying methods in this book and taking the night before the exam off from that subject. Don't even look at your notes or textbook for that class.

You probably think that I am out of my mind at this point, but I assure you I am not. The less stress and anxiety you feel about the subject, the better you will do on the exam. In addition, if you created a study/project timeline to know when you needed to read the text, completed assignments, and incorporated class notes into your study notes, you already know the required information. Cramming is just going to increase your stress and anxiety, so take the night off from studying anything for that class. Taking the night off doesn't mean just quickly review the class material. Take the morning or before class off too. Don't look at anything for the class 24 hours prior to the exam. In essence, this means to ignore that this class exists until the next day when you take the exam. Walk-in confident and know that all the information has slowly been implanted in your brain and is just waiting for you to retrieve it. Plus, the information will stay there longer and will be available in other classes and situations for you to pull from it.

Creating the study timeline will give you a clear plan of when you need to study each part of the class, help reduce anxiety, and ensure that you are ready for class each day. When you use the study timeline and calendar, you won't need to cram.

Breaks

Did you ever study so long your brain hurt, or you thought nothing else would stick? Well, there is a point where the brain does shut down and stops retaining information. What? You heard me. The brain will only work for so long before it needs a break.

Remember our calendar from the previous section? Notice that the Art class has two 30 minute study sessions. This is because your brain needs to take a break every 25 - 35 minutes. If you don't give it a break, it will stop retaining information. You will read the works and do the project, but the information won't stick.

SUNDAY

1:30pm - 2:00pm
English Study Time
2:00pm- 2:30pm
English Study Time

3:00pm - 3:30pm
Science Study Time
3:30pm - 4:00pm
Science Study Time

4:30pm - 5:00pm
History Study Time
5:00pm - 5:30pm
History Study Time

Therefore, you study for 30 minutes and then take a 5 to 7-minute break to reset the brain. Think of it like giving your eyes the 20-second rest from the computer screen every 20 minutes. What? Didn't you know that either? Well, you should give your eyes a break. This break reduces eye strain, which can lead to needing glasses. It is not an overnight kind of deal, but it builds up and hurts the eyes over time. But back to the brain. The brain needs 5 to 7 minutes to reset. This is a quick break to grab water, a non-sugar snack, and go to the bathroom. This is not a break to complete a video game's mission or to go out and shoot hoops. It is not a break to call up your bestie and talk clothes or listen to music. It is about taking a step away from the study space and book and recharging yourself briefly before getting back to studying.

When you are creating your study timeline, add the breaks. You also need to consider how long you will be studying each subject. Depending on where you are in your academic career, you may be able to study for 30 minutes on each subject and be fine, but that is not always the case. In our example, the student is studying one subject for an hour with a break in the middle. You should always try to study at the same time every day, but we all know that is not always possible. When it is not possible on a given day due to a job or appointment, change it in the calendar, but make it as close to the original time as possible. Keeping your study time consistent helps to build it as a habit, which in the end will help you have a more productive and efficient study time. In addition, you should study 6 days a week taking Saturday off. Why Saturday? We usually do not have classes on Sunday, and we will want to review for Monday's classes, so taking off Saturday makes more sense.

How do you feel about studying now? Creating a study space, knowing you can take breaks, you should not cram, and understanding the need to be able to schedule even study time should be making you see that a little extra upfront work will make your time during the school year much easier.

Now it is time to learn some study strategies that will make studying two hours a day more than enough.

Chapter 3: Study Strategy – Memorization

Memorization is one of the most important skills in your life. That's right, in life, not just in school. You will use your memory when going to the store on your way home from work. You will use your memory for work and home life. Memory is not something that is bound to the walls of your academic institution. It is a necessity of life. For this reason, keeping your memory strong and improving it are so important.

Consider this. How many times have you used your memory about an event or situation or compared a memory to something in the present to something in the last month? Week? Day? Hour? I can almost guarantee that you have used your memory quite recently, and I bet you did it without thinking about it. The only time we really think about it is when we have to delve deep to find what we were supposed to have remembered. Unfortunately, sometimes we never find it, which can be detrimental in school and at work. For those of you at work, how often have you had to remember something from a meeting or call, but you didn't write it down. Did you remember to do whatever it was you were supposed to remember? Or maybe someone asked you to take out the trash when you got home; did you remember?

I'm guessing most of us will answer these questions with a resounding, sometimes. Unless you have an eidetic or photographic memory, you would never say always. If you have this kind of memory, you are many steps ahead of the rest of us. For the rest of us, there are memorization hacks. I'm sure you have probably heard or used some of these hacks before without even thinking about them, but when you think about them, you realize they work. AND they work without having to delve deep into that abyss of the mind that sometimes loses things we were meant to remember.

The easiest way to improve your memory is to use mnemonic devices. Mnemonic what? Mnemonic devices (1st m is silent). These devices include acronyms, acrostics, rhymes, and method of loci. Not Loki, loci with a long i sound. Give me a few minutes, and I'll explain each to you.

Acrostic

An acrostic is very similar to an acronym, but instead of just using letters, you create a sentence using the first letter of each word of the phrase or list. The created sentences are usually silly, but the sentence is a memory cue that works.

One of the first acrostics most people learn is "My Very Educated Mother Just Served Us Nine Pizzas" or some similar variation. The first thing many people think of when they hear this are the planets in our solar system: Mercury, Venus, Earth, Mars, Jupiter, Saturn, Uranus, Neptune, Pluto. Unfortunately, with Pluto falling in and out of planet status, the acrostic continues to change, but even the first four words and we know.

How about some other ones? What are some acrostics you know? Here are some other acrostics that are relatively common.

- Please excuse, my dear Aunt Sally - used in math to teach the order of operations - parenthesis, exponents, multiply, divide, add, subtract.
- Roy G. Biv - used to remember the order of the colors in a rainbow - red, orange, yellow, green, blue, indigo, violet
- Here's one for Biology - King Phil Came Over For Genes Special. This is not as common, but it will help you in biology class. This represents the biology classification system - Kingdom, phylum, class, order, family, genus, species

How many of these did you know? Just think how much fun it will be to create your own silly sentences to help you remember lists and phrases for classes.

Acronym

The first one should be easy for most everyone. They are in our lives daily, mostly if we text. An acronym consists of letters where each letter represents the first letter of a given word. We sometimes even use the acronym instead of the actual phrase and never think twice about it. In fact, take a minute and write down some of the acronyms that you know and/or use daily - just 2 minutes and write as many of them down as you can. You can use many of these acronyms with anyone, and they will know exactly what you mean.

Acronym	Phrase
ASAP	as soon as possible
IDK	I don't know
SMH	shake my head
SCUBA	Self-Contained Underwater Breathing Apparatus
PEMDAS	parenthesis, exponents, multiply, divide, add, subtract

Did you know that SCUBA was an acronym? Yep, it is. It makes you wonder what other words we use daily are really acronyms. I say there are a few. Over time, when the acronym is used consistently it becomes part of speech, and it is more widely accepted than the actual phrase itself.

So how do you create an acronym? Take the phrase or list and create a group of letters. Let's use acronyms, acrostics, rhymes, and method of loci as an example. We could say A.A.R.M or say "aarm" (pronounced arm). It will not stick immediately, but if you use it consistently during studying, by the time the test rolls around, you will remember the four memorization devices. It is all about creating something to use consistently to help you remember.

Rhymes

Now onto rhymes. I bet you wondered why I didn't include the sentence, "In 1492, Columbus sailed the ocean blue" in the acrostic section? Well, that is because this sentence is not an acrostic but a rhyme. It is a silly sentence, but it rhymes. This mnemonic device is almost as fun as acrostics and does the same thing.

How about this one - "30 Days has September, April, June, and November. All the rest have 31, except February alone, which has but 28 days clear, and 29 in each leap year." Did you know it continued after the word February? Many of us don't know the whole rhyme, but we know enough to know which months have 30 days and which have 31 and that February is an outlier. In fact, this is a perfect example that shows we do not have to remember the entire sentence. We only have to remember the majority of it, and it will jog our memory and bring all the information up to the front of our brains.

Another example of a rhyme is the Alphabet Song. Did you realize we sing the alphabet to the melody of "Twinkle, Twinkle, Little Star"? Most people don't until someone mentions it, and then it is like, "Wow, it is!"

Sure, most of these rhymes are for children, but that doesn't mean you can't utilize this for your own needs. Maybe memorize facts to a favorite song. Or create a poem to help you remember a date or event. As long as you use it consistently, maybe even write it down too, you will always remember it.

Method of Loci

First, let's get pronunciation right. With the world of Avengers and Loki, I think this is important. Loci is pronoun (low - ki [long i sound]). And technically, a method of loci is just a study buddy. You are probably wondering if I am a person to study with, but that would defeat the purpose of studying. Has anyone ever really studied when they were studying with more people than on their own? A little studying may happen, maybe, but if we are honest, we weren't studying, really.

The method of loci or study buddy is a thing or location that you associate with a specific topic. If you study at home, maybe each room of the house is a method of loci. For example, the kitchen is all about science; the living room is about history, and so on. Each subject should have its own room. You can get jumbled if you use one room for multiple subjects.

To use a room, you visualize the area and associate information with items found in that room with what you are studying. Following the above example, when you are studying science and associate the kitchen with science, you would use items that you can readily see in the kitchen to attach to different topics and ideas you are studying in that class. For example, magnets on a refrigerator could be the classification system. It is all about what item helps you remember.

If you don't think using different rooms in the house will work, you can always have a trinket of some sort you have on the desk during the test. Make sure it is not electronic, cannot be written on, and is small. Different pens for different classes. A 6-sided die for science and a 10-sided die for math. A troll doll with different-colored hair for each class. Pick something different for each class. Make sure you have this item with you when studying the subject. Put it on the desk or table that is your study space while studying that subject. While you are in class, have it on your desk, so it is visible to you. This will set in motion that your memory will remember information about the class every time you see that object. The item has to be significant to you in relation to the subject so pick wisely.

Now that you have these memorization strategies, you can use A.A..R.M. to remember them, and you can think of how they will save you time and help you take tests more effectively. Try them out. See which one or ones work for you. Rhyming may work for history, but acronyms may be better for biology. Find the ones that resonate with you for each subject. The ones that are easiest to use for a subject are the ones that should be used for that subject. Mix and match and have fun with your memorization.

Chapter 4: Study Strategy – Reading Assignments

There are several ways to read your assignments and texts for your classes. Yes, you read that right. There is more than one way to read. Sometimes we read for pleasure. When reading this way, we can skim over dull areas and just read the important and sometimes fun stuff. However, we are taught that we have to read everything in each chapter of our textbooks when we are in school. We cannot skim over anything, or we might miss something. And in part, this is true. You need to read the textbook in a much deeper way than reading a novel, whether fiction or nonfiction. When reading like you are reading this book, you will retain some things, but not everything that is needed. Worse yet is that assignments and textbooks are not like books we read for pleasure. When reading for yourself, you will not remember the nuances and little details that will be important for final projects or for upcoming exams. You will remember the gist or overall topic of the book and may remember a few things, but you would have to look back at the chapters to find the details and refresh your memory on other details.

So how do you read your assignments and textbooks? Do you really read them or just skim them. How many times have you looked at due dates on an assignment but not the prompt or instructions? How many times have you gotten an answer wrong in class or on a test only to be told or find it in the textbook later? Most of us are guilty of this at least a few times. Personally, I would have had a life sentence if it were punishable with jail time. Luckily, I had another instructor who called me out on it on assignments and during class. You cannot say much when you answer a question wrong in the middle of a class lecture only to be asked if you "actually read the text assigned for that day" or "actually read the assignment prompt and instructions." Yep, those questions were the bane of my existence in two classes in my junior year of college. But there was hope for me, and there is hope for you.

This chapter will focus just on reading and understanding assignments. The following chapter will discuss how to read and better retain information from a textbook. So, let's get started.

Assignments

Most people think that reading an assignment is easy. Just read what the assignment says, note the due date, and be done with it. However, as you continue your academic career, the expectations become greater. What got you through middle school may get you through high school, but it will not give you a great GPA to get you into that college you want to attend. Understanding how to break down the assignment and the short deadlines is half the battle. It all starts with reading the assignment entirely and organizing it on a project timeline, and then entering the due dates in your calendar. We have already started to discuss this in Chapter 2: Calendar and Timelines, but we look at it differently in this chapter.

The first thing you need to do is go to Appendix B and read the assignment in its entirety.

Now that you are back, it seems like a clear-cut assignment, right? The instructor spelled everything out and left nothing to be confused about, right? You can now create your project timeline because you know all the steps you need to take, right?

Now answer the following questions without turning back to Appendix D:

- How many pages does the assignment require?
- What is the format you are to use?
- Do you need a video for a source?
- What is the topic?

Could you answer these four questions? The chances are that a few of you reading this could answer most of them; many of you reading this page looked back to answer most of them, and most of you just could not answer more than one of the questions. If you read the assignment correctly, you would have been able to answer all the questions. If you had written each part of the essay that was due on a project timeline, then you would definitely have known the answer to each question and more. Why? Because you not only read the information, but you wrote it out and started to memorize pieces because you read it and wrote it. All these things work in conjunction with each other.

Grab a project timeline or a piece of paper to use for this exercise, and let's work through this. Many of you are in high school, so your timelines may be different, or the way the teacher gives the assignment may not look like this; however, you should have some semblance of this for your assignment.

The first thing we want to do is write down the Final Assignment and due date, then all subsequent assignments and associated due dates on your project timeline. You should include how and when the assignments are to be submitted. Should the assignment be submitted in hard copy and/or electronically? At what time does the assignment become "late" to the instructor? You need to know these things. For this assignment, the Final Assignment is due as a hard copy and in the online classroom by 4 pm on December 5th. Now we work backwards, adding in the other steps with due dates to ensure we do not miss anything. The conference with the instructor will be Small Assignment 1, the rough draft will be Small Assignment 2, the peer review is Small Assignment 3, and Outline will be Small Assignment 4. Remember to include the due date and how each small assignment should be submitted to the instructor.

EXAMPLE

Final Assignment: <u>8-10 page double spaced paper in APA format.</u> <u>The reference sheet and Title page are not included in the page count.</u>

<u>I can use only 8 quotes in total. There must be 12 academic credible sources to include 2 videos (one of which is the MLK Jr. "I Have a Dream" speech), 3 other sources of my choosing, and 7 scholarly journals. I have to write in an academic tone and ensure my paper is free of grammatical errors and spelling errors. This will need time to research and create a logical, organized, well-thought-out research essay proving the point of my chosen topic and stance.</u>

Deadline: <u>December 5 by 4pm in hard copy to the professor's office and on Blackboard</u>

EXAMPLE

Small Assignment #1: <u>Conference with Professor</u>
Small Assignment #2: <u>Rough draft Submission</u>
Small Assignment #3: <u>Prepare a draft for in-class peer review</u>
Small Assignment #4: <u>Prepare an outline with a thesis statement for submission</u>

Remember, the more detail you include in your project timeline, the less you have to remember.

After you have the Small Assignments on the timeline, add the steps to help you reach the due dates with time to spare. Always include wiggle room so that you will still have time to get your assignment in on time if something happens unexpectedly.

Now that you have the assignments and associated due dates on the timeline, let's delve deeper into the actual assignment. When creating the timeline, we can cut and paste most of this information and not really read it. By doing that we may not give the instructor what is required. We want a good grade, so an in-depth reading of the assignment is needed.

The Topic

The instructor probably went over the assignment in class and gave clarifying instructions if anyone seemed confused or if someone asked a question; however, for the most part, all the information should be included on the assignment sheet. The first thing to look at then is the topic. For this assignment, the prompt is as follows:

Prompt: Choose your presentation carefully because you cannot change it. You need to decide if you will argue for a proposed solution to the problem with your topic or if you will argue about an ethical dilemma created by your topic. The purpose of the essay (proposal or ethical) needs to be shown in the introduction and thesis of your essay. How and from what perspective you write about your topic is up to you, but you have to create a logical, organized, well-thought-out research essay proving your point to do well on this paper. Do not try to cram it all in at the last minute. You have to take the time to complete this project appropriately. Everything (except the peer review) is part of the grade for this essay. Missing one piece will lower your grade.

You need to pick one of the topics below and start researching. You are not just listing facts or definitions. You must present your proposal or ethical argument in the accepted structure and remember to include the opposing side.

Possible topic – where you go with the topic is up to you:

- Freedom of Speech
- Freedom of Press
- Freedom of Religion

What is the topic? Not all instructors will give you an option, but in this example, you have six options. You are probably looking at the three bullet points and wondering why you are reading this book because the author is obviously crazy. Well, go up to the middle of the first paragraph of the "Prompt." It says, "...you will argue for a proposed solution to the problem with your topic or ... you will argue about an ethical dilemma created by your topic." Therefore, you have two options for each of the three bullet points, which gives six possible topic options. You would be able to narrow it down even more, but basically, there are six options. For example, Student A may want to give a solution to a problem he/she sees with the Freedom of Religion, but Student B wants to look at whether the Freedom of Religion causes an ethical dilemma for a specific religion. Both students are writing about Freedom of Religion, but they are looking at them in two different ways.

Now that we have our topic let's clarify it on our project timeline Final Assignment section. You do this by creating a working thesis statement that states the topic of your essay.

The Purpose

Next, we need to understand the purpose of this paper. Assignments are always way more than just the prompt or topic. What is the purpose of this assignment?

Purpose: Throughout the semester, you have written various types of arguments, considered multiple viewpoints on your specific topic, and formulated your arguments concerning your topic. You have supported your thesis statements with sound evidence, reasoning, and rhetorical appeals. In addition, you have used library and online research strategies to find reliable sources. This assignment will encompass all the writing, critical thinking, and information literacy skills you have developed during this course. Your essay will show that you can meaningfully engage in issues with civic and/or global relevance.

Let's break it down. The statement, "This assignment will encompass all the writing, critical thinking, and information literacy skills you have developed during this course" is the first part of the purpose. The writing and critical thinking skills are what you have learned with every paper written before this final project. These skills were honed with every mistake you have corrected and every way you thought about an argument and presented it logically. For the information literacy skills, the purpose is about understanding and being able to complete library and online research and using that researched information to support your evidence and thesis. Technically the purpose is to show what you have learned and how your understanding has grown since the first assignment. Now update your Final Assignment section of the timeline to include the purpose of this paper with one sentence.

How can we show our understanding of the topic? By following all the instructions and utilizing all the knowledge of writing and critical thinking. The rest of what we need is given to us in the assignment.

The Sources

In academic writing, we often use sources to prove our point. These sources have to meet specific criteria, and sometime during the class, the instructor would have had lectures and assignments to help you understand what a credible source is and how to use it. For this assignment, the instructor has even told the students what types of sources to use: scholarly journals, videos, and other credible sources. Write on the Final Assignment line the breakdown of sources.

The Evaluation

Most instructors will give a rubric to the students so that they understand what is expected if the students want to get an "A" on the paper. This usually is broken down and points given to each part of the evaluation could encompass organization of the essay, grammar, sources, formatting, clarity and cohesiveness, and other items depending on the purpose of the essay. For this assignment, the rubric can be found in their online classroom, Blackboard. Always make sure you have a hard copy of it and keep it with you always so you can understand how the instructor will grade, and you can gauge your essay against it when you are writing and editing it.

The Essay Requirements

Now, we will look at the essay requirements. In most instances, these are often given in detail.

Essay Requirements:

- Length: 8- 10 double-spaced type pages
- Tone/Stance: Academic/scholarly tone
- 12 academic credible sources required
- Format: **APA Manuscript Format**
  1. Title page, typed 12 pt. font is Times New Roman; In-text citations; Reference page (Title page and Reference page not included in page count).
- The essay must have a clear thesis statement – clear stance on the issue in the introduction paragraph
- The essay must have a clear organization – grouping of ideas and order of ideas.
- The essay must be free of grammatical and spelling errors
- Use **no more than 8 quotes total** within this paper from any source.
- The essay **must include APA in-text citation and a Reference page – failure to meet this requirement will result in an automatic "F" for the essay.**

In this example, we know how long the paper should be, how to format the paper, what tone we should use, and who our audience is. It also gives a limit on the number of quotes allowed and how to get an "F." You want to make sure that all of these items are on your Final Assignment section so that you can use the section as a checklist before you submit your final draft.

Our Final Assignment section should now look similar to the following:

Final Assignment:

*The Freedom of Religion is a fundamental basic right given to the American people in the US Constitution; however, at times this right has created friction and been misused for purposes that are not religious at all.

* I am to prove my point by utilizing the library and online research and writing an essay that uses critical thinking and association.

* There must be 12 academic credible sources to include 2 videos (one of which is the MLK Jr. "I Have a Dream" speech), 3 other sources of my choosing, and 7 scholarly journals.

*Check against the class rubric

* 8-10 page double spaced paper in APA format.

* Reference sheet and Title page are not included in page count. *

* I can use no more than 8 quotes total. I have to write in an academic tone and ensure my paper is free of grammatical errors and spelling errors.

* I will need time to research and create a logical, organized, well-thought-out research essay proving the point of my chosen topic and stance.

While we had most of the information in the original Final Assignment section, we have clarified it further to be able to use it as a checklist before submitting our essay. Before you submit your essay in person or online, you should always revisit the assignment and double-check that you have fulfilled the requirements listed in the Assignment description. If you haven't touched all the essay requirements, go back and add the part or parts that are missing.

From my teaching experience, I know that this last step is crucial. There is nothing worse than having points taken off or dropping from an "A" to a "B" because you forgot the Reference page, your page count was wrong, or you didn't use a specific type of source. It is horrible for the student, but it is also horrible for the professor especially when he/she told you what they expected, and you didn't take the time to read the instructions and follow them.

Remember, college is not just giving you an academic career. College is building your skills to take on a job that is based on your academic experience. Think about it this way. If an employer or supervisor gives you a project with a specific due date, you are expected to complete the project as instructed by a specific date. Right? What happens if you don't follow instructions or are missing a piece of the project? You may be removed from the project, written up, or if this is not the first time you didn't fulfill expectations of your role and/or project, you may be fired. Think of assignments as honing your skills for the job you are so excited to start upon graduation, and it will make the due dates and instructions much more relatable to real-world knowledge.

Now let's move away from reading assignments and learn the best, most efficient way to read your textbooks.

Chapter 5: Study Strategy – Reading Textbooks

You've made it to the section where you will learn to read your textbooks more efficiently and in less time. Why is this important? Because no one wants to read the textbook. OK, slight exaggeration. Most people do not want to read every single word in a textbook. I know I didn't whether I was a student or professor. Yes, professors read the textbooks they use in class, so while they don't have to read it every time they teach the class, they do have to read it every time the department changes to a new edition or a new text.

Anyway, this is not about how professors and teachers have to read the text, but how you have to read the text and figure out what is important and what is not. How can we know the teacher's brain, right? Well, that part is pretty easy, but before we get there, let's look at the best way to read the text, and then the answer about knowing the teacher's brain will be answered.

I bet you have heard of SQR3 in your time as a student. Somewhere someone mentioned this to you. You may or may not remember what the acronym stands for, but I'll help you remember. SQR3 stands for Survey, Question, Read, Recite, Review. However, I am a firm believer that this is missing something. I reworked this just a little, and my students loved it. I use the SQR4 method, which includes Survey, Question, Read, Recite, Review but also incorporates Remember. Well, duh! If we do all this, we better remember. However, this is the part where we incorporate the teacher's brain into the equation that will help you focus on the areas of importance.

What does SQR4 do? It helps you understand and retain information from the textbook that you will need for quizzes and exams without reading every single word in the textbook. That's right. You can get everything you need without reading everything.

Survey

What do I mean by survey? Honestly, it is an easy answer. Using a single chapter that has been assigned, look at the titles, subtitles, and headings in that chapter, and think about what they mean to you regarding the course. Then read the questions at the end of the chapter. Most textbooks have these as a way to review the chapter. The great thing is that you don't have to answer the questions at the end of a chapter, just kind of look at them. Think of them as a type of guide. The titles, subtitles, headings in each chapter, and questions at the end of each chapter, are your map of the chapter. They tell you and help you gain a little more information on what is important to the author in this chapter.

Question

Now you are going to either take out your laptop, tablet, note cards, or pen and paper and make the chapter title into a question. Then you are going to take every subtitle, heading, pretty much anything that is in bold font or different color and pertaining to a new section, and make it into a question that you will answer.

On a computer, it is easy to move things around, but if you are using pen and paper, which is what I did, you will put the question at the top of the page and each page (front and back) is only one question. Will you use the front and back for one question? I don't know. It depends, so it is always better to leave a lot of extra space than not enough.

Read

Yes, now we have the dreaded reading part. I am sure many of you are making faces and thinking, she told us we didn't have to read. I agree that reading a text is so worth making an ugly face because it is usually extremely boring. But I never said you wouldn't have to read. I said you wouldn't have to read everything, and I stand by that. A little reading is necessary. But it is how you read that changes. Reading more effectively is the hack here.

Step 1 is to take the paper or screen that has the question of the first section after the introduction of the chapter that you created and place it in front of you. This would be the first bold or different color heading or subheading that stands out to you. Have it open and ready to complete. Now is the fun part.

If there is only 1 paragraph in the section, read the first 3rd of it and the last sentence. That should answer the question in general. The paragraph's main topic is in the beginning section and the closing sentence of the paragraph about 99% of the time. Sometimes authors like to change it up every so often, but a consistent textbook cannot be written in this way. Therefore, this works more than not. Once you read those few sentences, paraphrase them into one to three sentences and write this paraphrase down under your question.

If the section is more than one paragraph, the formula changes just a little. You will read the entire first paragraph and then the last two to three sentences of the last paragraph of the section. Again, the information in these areas will answer the question you created from the section heading. Now paraphrase the idea that answers the question and write it under the question.

Continue to do this for every question you created from subtitles and headings. The very last question you will answer is the question you created from the title of the chapter. Use the information you just answered all the other questions to create a paraphrased paragraph that answers the question and write it under the question.

Now you have not only answered all questions of topics that the author of the textbook thought was important, but you paraphrased the entire chapter without reading every word in that chapter. I guarantee you that you have more knowledge about the topic now, and it was interactive rather than boring - OK, as non-boring as working through a chapter in a textbook can be, but it wasn't just sitting and reading. It was interactive.

Remember, if this part takes longer than 30 minutes, get up and take your break. Part of the reading step will be retained, and we want to retain as much as possible.

Recite

Now you have notes on a computer, sheet of paper, or flashcards to use to study that talk about everything in the chapter. I would suggest printing the notes from the computer, so you have a hard copy. If the answers are short, you can put the question on one side and the answer on the other to create flashcards. You could also set up a Cornell Notes template on the computer or sheet of paper and put the questions and answers in the document that way. Again, if you do this on a computer, print it out. No matter what, you just have to find what works for you. You also have to consider that what works in one class may not work as well in another class, so play around with how you create the questions and answers to use in this step.

If you feel really industrious or want a little more study help, you can also answer the questions at the end of the chapter. However, before you do, read them again, and I bet many of them coincide with questions you created from the titles, subtitles, and headings. Answering more questions will not help you retain more information.

You have your notes and/or flashcards in front of you so that you can quiz yourself. Ask the question out loud, and then answer the question out loud. Saying things out loud helps to reinforce the idea or information into your brain.

Review

This is the easiest part of SQR4. Review your notes every day. Add more pages or flashcards as more chapters from the textbook are added before each exam. Once you have taken the exam on those chapters, you can probably put the notes aside until closer to the final, if the final is comprehensive. If it is not comprehensive, then the notes have fulfilled their purpose once you are done with the exam.

Remember

However, we have one more step before the exam that we have to incorporate into our SQR4 process, and it is how to know the instructor's brain. It is almost 99% guaranteed that if the teacher emphasizes something during the class lecture, it will be on a test. That is the secret.

You want to complete the first 5 steps (SQR3) before the lecture on that chapter. You should do this for several reasons. First, if you get called on in class, then you can answer the question. Second, if you create questions and answer them before the class lectures, then you will be able to go back to those sections the instructor discussed and emphasized during class and add the class notes to those question pages or flashcards.

If you feel like you are still missing pieces of these emphasized lecture sections, read the questions at the end of the chapter and answer them. However, your questions, paraphrased answers, and the notes from the class lecture should be all you need to answer those questions, feel confident that you have the information you need from the textbook, and have the ability to ace the exam.

Chapter 6: F.O.C.U.S.

Well, you are almost done. You are now a step ahead of most of your student peers. You have the knowledge of being more effective and efficient in your studying and thereby allowing yourself to have a life while maintaining your GPA. This is especially true if you have obligations and responsibilities outside of the academic environment. We all need ways of doing things more effectively and in less time, so let this be a guide.

F.O.C.U.S. is an acronym to help you remember all that you have learned and that you should put into place to give you a stronger study foundation in all classes. Some of these items or activities you only have to do once, but they are just as important as those items that you have to do continuously. Now, let's review.

F - Find a good place to study. Remember that having a study space with fewer distractions is extremely important. This study space allows you to optimize the time you have to study, thereby decreasing the actual time you need for studying.

O - Organization. You need to get and stay organized. Create the calendar. Create project timelines. Yes, it takes a little more at the beginning of the semester, but it will add more free time to your schedule after that first week.

C- Concentrate. You need to practice the strategies that help you concentrate on the work you have to do and not your surroundings. Sounds easy, but it is not always as easy as we need or hope. Practice the strategies.

U - use mnemonic devices. A.A..R.M. What is this mnemonic? You should know it if you read the Memorization chapter.

S - SQR4 Reading Strategy. Yes, you still have to read, but by using this method, you will know what to read and how to figure out what is important to the instructor.

Now you are ready. Remember, while these work great in an academic setting, you can transfer them to a real-world setting in the office or workplace when you graduate. These skills are not just academic, but life skills that will help you in many ways throughout your lifetime.

Appendices

Appendix A – Student Contract Option 1

Appendix A – Student Contract

OPTION 1

I, Your Name Here, have concluded that I need 2 hours daily to sit quietly and study. I would like to do this every day, Monday through Friday from Time to Time. On Saturdays, it will be from Time to Time. I have created a study space at/in location of study space and would appreciate this area to be a quiet zone on those days and times. I will not leave my studying on the table but will bring it to the table 5 minutes before the scheduled time and remove it within 5 minutes at the end of the scheduled time.(ONLY USE THIS LINE IF YOU ARE STUDYING IN A PUBLIC SPACE IN THE HOUSE) I would also be willing to do chores before and/or after the scheduled time but would appreciate not being asked to do chores during the scheduled time. I feel that creating this study space and study schedule is being proactive in ensuring I have good grades throughout the school year. If you agree with my requested schedule, please sign below.

_________________________	_____________
Student	Date
_________________________	_____________
Family Member	Date
_________________________	_____________
Family Member	Date
_________________________	_____________
Family Member	Date
_________________________	_____________
Family Member	Date
_________________________	_____________
Family Member	Date

* Remember to add more signatures or remove them as needed for your home.

Appendix A – Student Contract Option 2

OPTION 2

I, Your Name Here, have come to the conclusion that I need 2 hours daily to sit quietly to study. I would like to do this every day, Monday through Friday from Time to Time. On Saturdays, it will be from Time to Time. I have created a study space at/ in location of study space and would appreciate this area to be a quiet zone on those days and times. I will not leave my studying on the table but will bring it to the table 5 minutes before the scheduled time and remove it within 5 minutes at the end of the scheduled time.(ONLY USE THIS LINE IF YOU ARE STUDYING IN A PUBLIC SPACE IN THE HOUSE). I feel that creating this study space and study schedule is being proactive in ensuring I have good grades throughout the school year and to help our family in the long run. If you agree with my requested schedule, please sign below.

Student	Date
Family Member/Roommate	Date
Family Member/Roommate	Date
Family Member/Roommate	Date
Family Member/Roommate	Date
Family Member/Roommate	Date

* Remember to add more signatures or remove them as needed for your home.

Appendix B - Writing Prompt and Project Timeline

Appendix B - Writing Prompt and Project Timeline

<u>WRITING PROMPT</u>
Researched Argument (30% of grade)

Prompt: Choose your presentation carefully because you cannot change it. You need to decide if you will argue for a proposed solution to the problem with your topic or if you will argue about an ethical dilemma created by your topic. The purpose of the essay (proposal or ethical) needs to be shown in the introduction and thesis of your essay. How and from what perspective you write about your topic is up to you, but you have to create a logical, organized, well-thought-out research essay proving your point to do well on this paper. Do not try to cram it all in at the last minute. You have to take the time to complete this project appropriately. Everything (except the peer review) is part of the grade for this essay. Missing one piece will lower your grade.

You need to pick one of the topics below and start researching. You are not just listing facts or definitions. You must present your proposal or ethical argument in the accepted structure and remember to include the opposing side.

Possible topic – where you go with the topic is up to you:

- Freedom of Speech
- Freedom of Press
- Freedom of Religion

Purpose: Throughout the semester, you have written various types of arguments, considered multiple viewpoints on your specific topic, and formulated your arguments in relation to your topic. You have supported your thesis statements with sound evidence, reasoning, and rhetorical appeals. In addition, you have used library and online research strategies to find reliable sources. This assignment will encompass all the writing, critical thinking, and information literacy skills you have developed during this course. Your essay will show that you can meaningfully engage in issues with civic and/or global relevance.

Sources: You need to use 12 sources for this essay. Of those 12 sources, 7 have to be scholarly journal (other than Opposing Viewpoints), 3 can be any other type of credible source, and 2 has to be video (1 can be a TedTalk or Interview on reputable site and 1 can be the "I Have a Dream" speech by Martin Luther King Jr.).

Evaluation: Your final essay will be evaluated using the Maryland Standards for a "C" in composition (found on Blackboard).

Due Date for Thesis & Outline: November 9 by midnight on Blackboard

Peer Review: November 14 in class with hard copy

Due Date for Rough Draft: November 21 at 4 pm hard copy and on Blackboard

Conference Dates: November 28 – December 2

Due Date for Final Essay: December 5 hard copy and on Blackboard

Essay Requirements:

- Length: 8- 10 double-spaced type pages
- Tone/Stance: Academic/scholarly tone
- 12 academic credible sources required
- Format: **APA Manuscript Format**
    ◦ Title page, typed 12 pt. font is Times New Roman; In-text citations; Reference page (Title page and Reference page not included in page count).
- The essay must have a clear thesis statement – clear stance on the issue in the introduction paragraph
- The essay must have a clear organization – grouping of ideas and order of ideas.
- The essay must be free of grammatical and spelling errors
- Use **no more than 8 quotes total** within this paper from any source.
- The essay **must include APA in-text citation and a Reference page – failure to meet this requirement will result in an automatic "F" for the essay.**

<u>SAMPLE PROJECT TIMELINE</u>

Instructions: The final assignment should encompass all the assignment requirements so that you can verify all have been met prior to submissions. The final assignment's deadline is the Final Assignment Due Date and Time when applicable. Remember, life can interrupt, so we have to build in some wiggle room.

The next step is to complete Small Assignments 1, 2, & 3. Small Assignment 1 should be the last action you need to completed to move you toward the long-term goal. Include smaller steps to reach the Small Assignment. Small Assignment 2 is the step that follows Small Assignment 1. Again include smaller steps to reach the Small Assignment. Small Assignment 3 is the step that follows Small Assignment 2 and is the final step before you reach the Final Assignment. Again include smaller steps, but when each step of this Small Assignment is complete, you should have reached the long-term goal. Remember to add deadlines to each Small Assignment and to each step needed to complete to reach that Small Assignment.

*NOTE: This activity should only focus on one Final Assignment. A separate Project Time Line should be completed for each project/assignment that you are given.

Final Assignment: 8-10 page double spaced paper in APA format. The reference sheet and Title page are not included in the page count. I can use no more than 8 quotes in total. There must be 12 academic credible sources to include 2 videos (one of which is the MLK Jr. "I Have a Dream" speech), 3 other sources of my choosing, and 7 scholarly journals. I have to write in an academic tone and ensure my paper is free of grammatical errors and spelling errors. This will need time to research and create a logical, organized, well-thought-out research essay proving the point of my chosen topic and stance.

Deadline: December 5 by 4pm in hard copy to the professor's office and on Blackboard

STEPS TO GET TO FINAL ASSIGNMENT

Small Assignment #1: Conference with Professor

Step 1 to reach Small Assignment #1: Complete all other assignments
Deadline for Step 1: November 21

Step 2 to reach Small Assignment #1: Sign up for the conference as soon as she opens up the conference times
Deadline for Step 2: November 21

Step 3 to reach Small Assignment #1: Attend the conference to discuss edits for my paper
Deadline for Step 3: November 28 at 2 pm

 Small Assignment #2: Rough draft Submission

Step 1 to reach Small Assignment #2: Use the peer reviewed paper to make edits
Deadline for Step 1: November 18

Step 2 to reach Small Assignment #2: Schedule an appointment at the Writing Center & make edits
Deadline for Step 2: November 19

Step 3 to reach Small Assignment #2: Submit the Rough Draft to the professor in hardcopy and on Blackboard
Deadline for Step 3: November 21 by 4pm

Small Assignment #3: Prepare a draft for in-class peer review

Step 1 to reach Small Assignment #3: Write a draft of my essay from my outline
Deadline for Step 1: November 11

Step 2 to reach Small Assignment #3: Schedule an appointment at the Writing Center & make edits
Deadline for Step 2: November 12

Step 3 to reach Small Assignment #3: Participate in Peer Review
Deadline for Step 3: November 14 in class

Small Assignment #4: Prepare an outline with a thesis statement for submission

Step 1 to reach Small Assignment #4: Research and choose my topic
Deadline for Step 1: November 1

Step 2 to reach Small Assignment #4: Schedule an appointment at the Writing Center
Deadline for Step 2: November 5

Step 3 to reach Small Assignment #4: Create my outline and thesis statement and include a basic reference sheet
Deadline for Step 3: November 7

Step 4 to reach Small Assignment #4: Schedule an appointment at the Writing Center
Deadline for Step 4: November 8

Step 5 to reach Small Assignment #4: Submit my outline, thesis statement, and references
Deadline for Step 5: November 9

Appendix C - Blank Project Timeline Template

Appendix C - Blank Project Timeline Template

Instructions: The final assignment should encompass all the assignment requirements so that you can verify all have been met prior to submissions. The final assignment's deadline is the Final Assignment Due Date and Time when applicable. Remember, life can interrupt, so we have to build in some wiggle room.

The next step is to complete Small Assignments 1, 2, & 3. Small Assignment 1 should be the last action you need to completed to move you toward the long-term goal. Include smaller steps to reach the Small Assignment. Small Assignment 2 is the step that follows Small Assignment 1. Again include smaller steps to reach the Small Assignment. Small Assignment 3 is the step that follows Small Assignment 2 and is the final step before you reach the Final Assignment. Again include smaller steps, but when each step of this Small Assignment is complete, you should have reached the long-term goal. Remember to add deadlines to each Small Assignment and to each step needed to complete to reach that Small Assignment.

*NOTE: This activity should only focus on one Final Assignment. A separate Project Time Line should be completed for each project/assignment that you are given.

Requirements and Deadline:

____

____

____

____

____

____

____

STEPS TO GET TO FINAL ASSIGNMENT

Small Assignment #1: _______________________________

____

____

____

Step 1 to reach Small Assignment #1: _______________________________

____

Deadline for Step 1: _______________________________

Step 2 to reach Small Assignment #1: _______________________________

Deadline for Step 2: _______________________________

Step 3 to reach Small Assignment 1#: _______________________________

Deadline for Step 3: _______________________________

Small Assignment #2: _______________________________

____

____

____

Step 1 to reach Small Assignment #2: _______________________________

____

Deadline for Step 1: _______________________________

Step 2 to reach Small Assignment #2: _______________________________

Deadline for Step 2: _______________________________

Step 3 to reach Small Assignment 2#: _______________________________

Deadline for Step 3: _______________________________

Small Assignment #3:___________________________________

____

____

____

Step 1 to reach Small Assignment #3: ______________________

____

Deadline for Step 1: ______________________

Step 2 to reach Small Assignment #3: ______________________

Deadline for Step 2: ______________________

Step 3 to reach Small Assignment 3#: ______________________

Deadline for Step 3: ______________________

Small Assignment #4: ______________________________

____

____

____

Step 1 to reach Small Assignment #4: ______________________

____

Deadline for Step 1: ______________________

Step 2 to reach Small Assignment #4: ______________________

Deadline for Step 2: ______________________

Step 3 to reach Small Assignment 4: ______________________

Deadline for Step 3: ______________________

REVIEWS FROM EXPERTS IN THE
FIELD

REVIEWS FROM EXPERTS IN THE FIELD

"As a writing professor, I think that this guide is a great way to help students stay on target in classes, assignments, and studying. As a writer, I am eager to see how to adapt her time management strategies for my own NANOWRIMO project."
   ---Dr. K. J. Robinson, Montgomery College, Germantown Campus

"I have watched my son apply Chanin's tips to his study habits and have seen him grow in confidence as a student. He used to struggle with school and writing. He now claims English as his favorite subject and feels much more confident as a student in general. I can't say enough good things about her study tips. I only wish I had them when I was a high school/college student!"
   ---H. E. Williams-Deise, Parent of College Freshman

This is a must read for any student confused by all the rules out there! The information provided is practical advice, for the average student wanting to improve upon their academic journey as well as the challenged student who cannot focus to save their life. This step-by-step illustration of the simple mastery of studying is pure genius brought down to the level for common folk to comprehend! Well done!
   ---D. Sparks, Educator & Curriculum Designer

www.ingramcontent.com/pod-product-compliance
Lightning Source LLC
Chambersburg PA
CBHW030828060726
47590CB00004B/1450